Beautiful Etudes

Artistic Music that Promotes Technical Development at the Piano

Selected and Edited by **Victoria McArthur**

Alfred

2

Foreword

ᏽ TO TEACHERS

Etudes have provided pianists with valuable technical
training for generations. Today's pianists have more
demands on their time than ever before, therefore,
the materials chosen for study should be of the
highest musical quality, worthy of the time
expenditure. The pieces in *Beautiful Etudes* have
been tested and chosen by piano students and
teachers not only for their technical effectiveness but
also because they are lovely musical works.

ᏽ UNIQUE FEATURES

- 16 artistic studies
- Arranged in progressive order of difficulty
- Written in accessible keys

ᏽ OTHER FEATURES

- Technical goals for each etude
- Composer biographical information
- Practice directions for each etude
- Suggested keys for transposition
- Creative suggestions for further musical
  and technical exploration
- Mastery and memorization checklists
- Glossary

ᏽ SUGGESTIONS FOR TEACHERS

- Play each etude for the student. Modeling of
  expressive playing is essential to convey musical
  and technical ideals.
- Provide concrete practice steps for the student,
  including slow, hands-separate practice
  with a metronome.

dedicated to
Caitlin, Erika and Stephany

Table of Contents

NOTE: Most titles are editorial.

BEFORE YOU PLAY

- Tap the rhythm hands together on your lap, counting aloud (first, subdivide for the eighth note, then for the quarter note).
- Circle, then block ("play" together) the chords created from the first three RH notes of the piece. Then, circle and block other similar chord patterns in measures 1–6. *Hint:* Look for the first three notes of the rhythm pattern

AS YOU PLAY

- Be careful of the many dynamic and articulation changes.
- Listen carefully to play the opening section (measures 1–8, beat 1) with a bright, confident tone in the RH, supported by a strong LH.

TRANSPOSE

- *Bold Spirit* is written in B♭ major.
- Transpose measures 10–20 (beat 1) to D major.
  Think: F is which scale degree in B♭ major?_____ Therefore, in D, the same scale degree is _____. This is your starting note.

CREATE

Make up a story for *Bold Spirit* and call it *The Wild Stallion.* Make sure that the motives at measure 1, measure 8, and measure 16 fit the story.

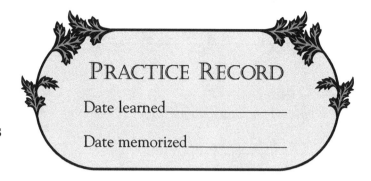

PRACTICE RECORD

Date learned_____

Date memorized_____

omposer Facts

Johann Christian Bach (1735–1782), German, was one of several sons of the great Johann Sebastian Bach (1685–1750). J. C. Bach, like his father, became a renowned composer. *Bold Spirit* is from the Francesco Pasquale Ricci Piano Method, published in Paris in 1788. It is unclear whether J. C. Bach actually composed this work, or whether Ricci may only have dedicated the piece to his friend's memory.

Bold Spirit

Johann Christian Bach

BEFORE YOU PLAY

- On the closed key cover, slowly "play" hands together. Give special attention to the *legato* LH melody in measures 5–12 (and similar places) and the *legato* RH in measures 13–20.

- Block the LH in measures 29–33.

AS YOU PLAY

- Listen for crisp RH staccato notes (played from the hand, not the arm) in measures 5–11.

- Make the LH two-note slur gestures in measures 13–19 very small. Do not lift high for the release at the end of each slur. Use a finger release, not an arm release.

TRANSPOSE

- *The Chase* is written in _____ _____.

- Transpose the LH of measures 44 (beat 6) through measure 56 to B major.

CREATE

Play measures 5–7, measures 9–11, and similar places, as:

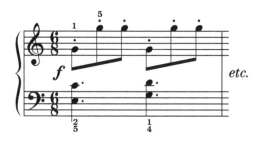

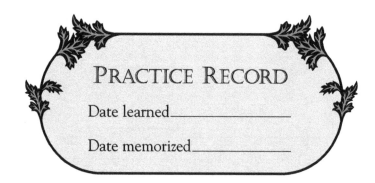

Johann Friedrich Burgmüller (1806–1874), German, wrote music that was quite popular in Paris society where his playing was also highly regarded. His melodic piano studies have been a significant part of the teaching repertoire since the time they were written, and are excellent preparation for the more difficult works of the Romantic Period.

The Chase

Op. 100, No. 9

Johann Friedrich Burgmüller

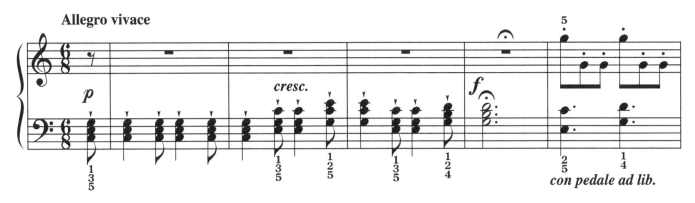

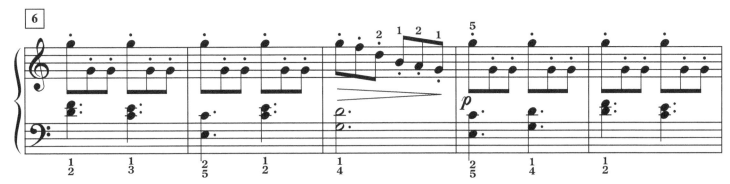

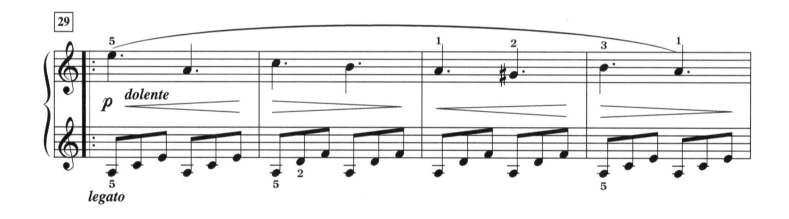

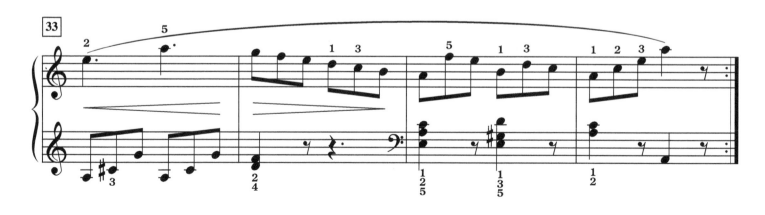

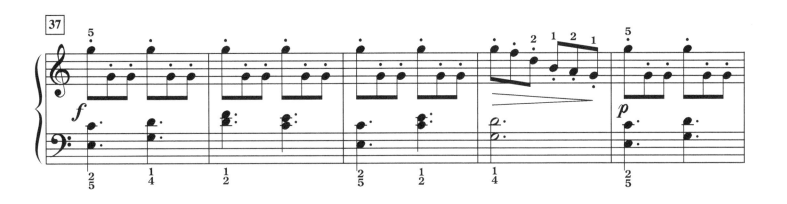

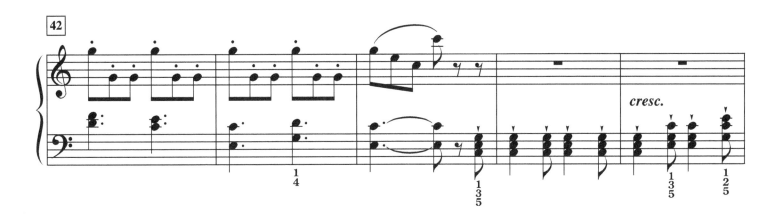

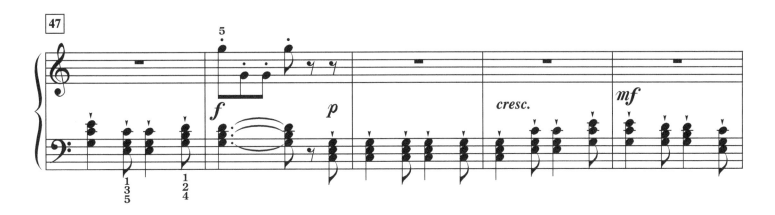

🎵 BEFORE YOU PLAY

- On the closed key cover, "play" hands together.
- Identify the cadence chords:

    1. Measures 1 (beat 4)–2:
        a. V I
        b. I V^7 *(circle one)*

    2. Measures 3 (beat 4)–4:
        a. V I
        b. V^7 I *(circle one)*

🎵 AS YOU PLAY

- For the arpeggios, do not twist the wrist as the RH thumb passes under. *Hint:* "Glide" the entire arm up the keyboard as though it were on rollers.
- Shape the RH five-note accompaniment figure in measures 9–16 with a small *crescendo* and *diminuendo* for each:

🎵 TRANSPOSE

- *High Jinks* is written in _____ minor.
- Transpose measures 1–8 to G minor.

🎵 CREATE

Vary the rhythms of the triplet figures.

Measures 1–8 and measures 19–24:

long short short   long short short   etc.

Measures 9–17:

long short short   long short short   etc.

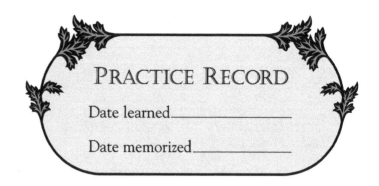

PRACTICE RECORD

Date learned_____

Date memorized_____

Composer Facts

Cornelius Gurlitt (1820–1901), German, was an organist, teacher and student of the composer Carl Reinecke (1824–1910). Best known as a composer, Gurlitt authored over 250 works, many of which continue to be played today.

High Jinks

Op. 141, No. 14

Cornelius Gurlitt

BEFORE YOU PLAY

On the closed key cover, "play" hands separately.

AS YOU PLAY

• Listen so that the LH notes on beat 1 of each measure sound like a secondary melody that supports the singing RH melody.

• "Shape" the melody carefully by making the last note of each phrase softer.

TRANSPOSE

• *Homage to Chopin* is written in _____ minor.

• Transpose measures 1–16 to E major, the parallel major key, hands separately. What are the sharps? ____ ____ ____ ____

CREATE

• Change the 𝅗𝅥 𝅘𝅥 RH rhythms to 𝅘𝅥 𝅗𝅥

• Change the 𝅘𝅥 𝅘𝅥 𝄽 LH rhythms to 𝅘𝅥 𝅘𝅥 𝅘𝅥 (same notes on beat 3 as on beat 2)

omposer Facts

Cornelius Gurlitt (1820–1901), *see page 10.*

Homage to Chopin

Op. 132, No. 1

Cornelius Gurlitt

 **BEFORE YOU PLAY**

- On the closed key cover, slowly "play" hands together.

- How many times does this rhythm pattern occur?

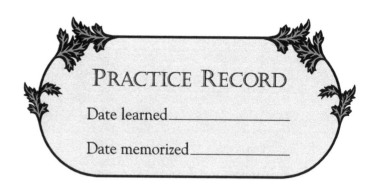

PRACTICE RECORD

Date learned_____

Date memorized_____

 **AS YOU PLAY**

- Look at the following dramatic points in the piece. List the musical features that add to the "drama." (*Examples:* rhythm, dynamics, number of notes, repetition)

  Measure 43_____

  _____

  Measures 51–61_____

  _____

- Locate spots where you play softly.

TRANSPOSE

- *Russian Dance* is written

  in _____ _____.

- Transpose measures 1–10 to E minor.

CREATE

Play the same notes with a new RH rhythm for measures 3–10.

Example:

etc.

Composer Facts

Hugo Reinhold (1854–1935), Austrian, was a pianist and composer noted for his energetic and popular piano pieces. He taught at the Vienna Conservatory of the Society of Friends of Music. Among his other compositions were works for orchestra, chorus, string quartet, and voice.

Russian Dance

Op. 39, No. 24

Hugo Reinhold

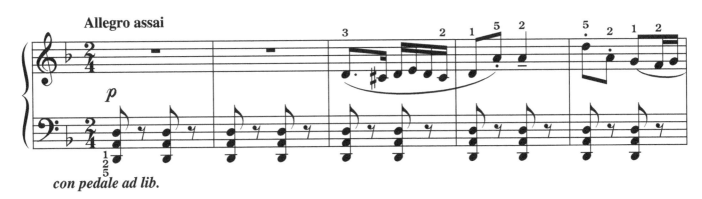

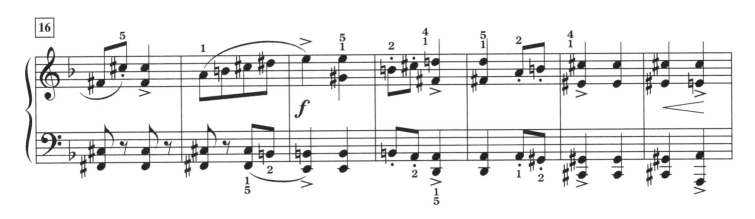

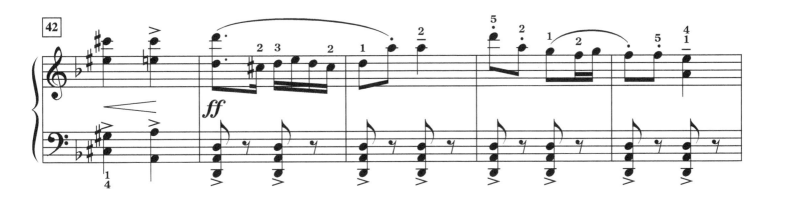
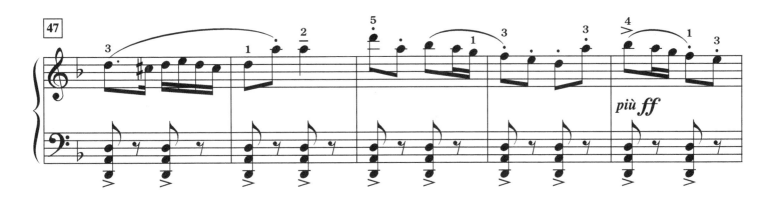

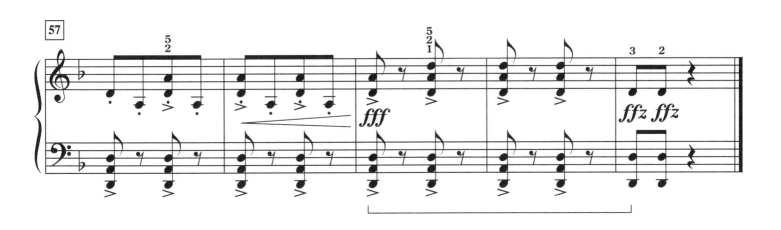

◈ BEFORE YOU PLAY

- Tap the rhythm (no trills) hands together, counting aloud.
- On the closed key cover, "play" hands together with no trills.

◈ AS YOU PLAY

- After you can play smoothly with no trills, add the trills. Listen so they start exactly on (not before) the beat.
- Let the arm glide for the arpeggios. Do not twist the wrist.

◈ TRANSPOSE

- *Grand Entrance* is written in _____ _____.
- Transpose measures 1–6 (beat 3) to C minor.
  Hint: For each arpeggio, write a Roman numeral on the music before transposing.

◈ CREATE

Write at least four more dynamic markings of your own, or change some that are already written. Play the piece with your new dynamics.

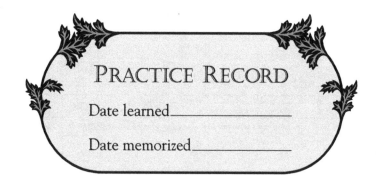

PRACTICE RECORD

Date learned_____

Date memorized_____

omposer Facts

Domenico Gasparini (1695–1743), Italian, was a composer and harpsichordist. He may possibly have been a son of noted composer, Francesco Gasparini (1668–1727), who was the teacher of Domenico Scarlatti (1685–1757) and Benedetto Marcello (1686–1739). Domenico Gasparini wrote harpsichord studies and sonatas that resemble those of Scarlatti.

Grand Entrance

Domenico Gasparini

✍ BEFORE YOU PLAY

- Locate and tap the melody, counting aloud.
  Note: The melody changes from RH to LH.

- On the closed key cover, slowly "play"
  hands together.

✍ AS YOU PLAY

To "shape" each phrase, find the most
important note in each phrase and
highlight it expressively with your playing.
Lightly mark an X over the most important
note for each phrase. For example, in
measures 10–17, the most important note
in each LH phrase is the half note.

✍ TRANSPOSE

- *Miniature Waltz* is written in B minor.

- Transpose measures 1–10 (beat 1)
  to A minor. Play hands separately,
  if needed.

✍ CREATE

Imagine that *Miniature Waltz* is being played
by a symphony orchestra. What instruments
(other than piano) can you imagine playing?

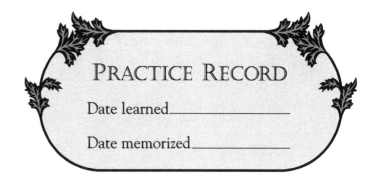

PRACTICE RECORD

Date learned_____

Date memorized_____

omposer Facts

Vladimir Rebikov (1866–1920), Russian,
sometimes is called the father of modern
Russian music. He lived in Berlin, Vienna,
and Moscow, where he frequently performed
piano concerts. Two of his favorite
compositional techniques were whole-tone
scales and parallel fifths.

Miniature Waltz

Op. 10, No. 10

Vladimir Rebikov

◦ BEFORE YOU PLAY

- Tap the rhythm hands together and count aloud.

- On the closed key cover, slowly "play," hands together.

◦ AS YOU PLAY

- Listen carefully to "voice" (bring out) the melody, especially in the three-note and four-note chords.

- Your playing should sound joyous and patriotic.

◦ TRANSPOSE

- *Rule Britannia* is written in _____ _____.

- Transpose measures 1–8 (beat 1) down a half step.
  Hint: Imagine a flat in front of every note except for F♯, which becomes F.

◦ CREATE

Play both hands an octave higher and *piano*. Describe how these changes affect the mood of the piece. _____

_____

_____

_____

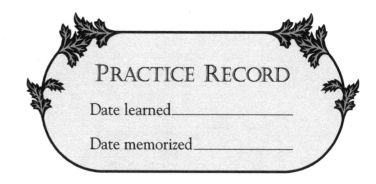

PRACTICE RECORD

Date learned_____

Date memorized_____

omposer Facts

Carl Czerny (1791–1857), Austrian, was a composer, a student of Ludwig van Beethoven (1770–1827), and the teacher of Franz Liszt (1811–1886). He was a famous virtuoso pianist who is best remembered for his thousands of exercises for piano.

Rule Britannia

(from *First Instructional Pieces*)

Carl Czerny

BEFORE YOU PLAY

On the closed key cover, "play" the RH alone, then both hands together.

AS YOU PLAY

- Listen for a light, lilting sound until measure 12 where the drama starts, then builds through measure 14.
- Avoid any breaks in the smooth scales when fingers cross over or under.

TRANSPOSE

- *Innocence* is written in ____ _____.
- Transpose measures 1–8 to G major. Does any fingering need to change for the new key?

CREATE

Create an excellent finger warm-up by changing the even sixteenth notes in measure 1 and similar places to a "long-short" rhythm.

Example:

long short long short long short long short

PRACTICE RECORD

Date learned_____

Date memorized_____

omposer Facts

Johann Friedrich Burgmüller (1806–1874), *see page 6.*

Innocence

Op. 100, No. 5

Johann Friedrich Burgmüller

BEFORE YOU PLAY

On the closed key cover, "play" all the sixteenth note passages. Be careful of the fingering.

AS YOU PLAY

• Listen for evenness in the chromatic scales. The thumb should not play loudly.

• Lighten your touch on the sixteenth notes, especially when played up to tempo.

TRANSPOSE

• *The Whirlwind* is written in _____ _____.

• Transpose measures 9–23 to G major.

CREATE

Make *The Whirlwind* sound humorous by writing *rit., accel.,* and *a tempo* where you wish. Call it *The Mosquitos.* Play your new version.

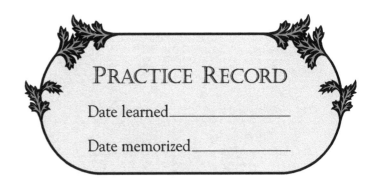

PRACTICE RECORD

Date learned_____

Date memorized_____

Composer Facts

Jean Louis Streabbog (1835–1886), Belgian, was actually Jean Louis Gobbaerts. ("Streabbog" is "Gobbaerts" spelled backwards.) Gobbaerts wrote under several other pen names, including Lecocq, Ludovic and Levy. He is best known for his piano salon pieces.

The Whirlwind

Op. 64, No. 9

Jean Louis Streabbog

✏ BEFORE YOU PLAY

- On the closed key cover, "play" each hand separately.
- On the keyboard, silently "block" as many LH notes as possible before moving your hand to a new "block."

✏ AS YOU PLAY

- Listen for the melody as it moves from LH to RH, or from RH to LH.
- Starting at measure 9, pay careful attention to the articulation marks and accents.

✏ TRANSPOSE

- *Happy Farmer* is written in _____ _____.
- Transpose the LH of measures 1–14 (beat 3) to E major.

✏ CREATE

Make up words about a *Happy Farmer* to fit the melody.

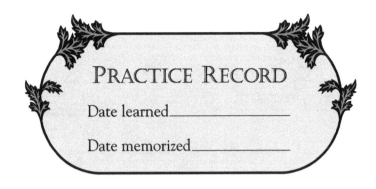

PRACTICE RECORD

Date learned_____

Date memorized_____

omposer Facts

Robert Schumann (1810–1856), German, was a composer, pianist, lawyer, and a noted writer and editor of literary essays. Schumann's imaginative compositions encompassed large cycles of works for piano, orchestral music, chamber music, choral and dramatic works, plus many songs and song-cycles. Schumann suffered from many physical and psychological ailments throughout his life. Late in Schumann's life and after his death, his wife Clara (1819–1896) carried on the family name as a pianist and composer in her own right.

Happy Farmer

Op. 68, No. 10

Robert Schumann

Frisch und munter (brisk and jolly)

✎ BEFORE YOU PLAY

- On the closed key cover, "play" hands together.
- Name the scales:

  Measure 1 _____ _____

  Measure 3 _____ _____

  Measure 5 _____ _____

  Measure 9 _____ _____

  Measure 11_____ _____

✎ AS YOU PLAY

- Listen for sparkling, bold scales, with all unison notes sounding exactly together.
- Be careful of the sudden dynamic changes. Circle the markings, if needed.

✎ TRANSPOSE

- *The Cadets* is written in B♭ major.
- Transpose to B major.
  Hint: Think the key signature for B major (5 sharps), or imagine each note a half step higher than written. Pay careful attention when accidentals occur. Remember to raise them a half step.

✎ CREATE

Play descending (not ascending, as written) scales in measures 1, 3, 5–7, 9 and 11.

Example:

PRACTICE RECORD

Date learned_____

Date memorized_____

Jean Louis Streabbog (1835–1886),
see page 26.

The Cadets

Op. 64, No. 11

Jean Louis Streabbog

❧ BEFORE YOU PLAY

- On the closed key cover, block ("play" together) the RH broken chords in measures 1–16.

- On the keyboard, play the RH melody alone, listening for an expressive, yet carefully controlled melodic shape.

- On the keyboard, play the melody with the RH, while the LH plays the other notes that are written in the treble. Listen for a singing RH melody, soaring over the murmuring LH.

❧ AS YOU PLAY

- Take care not to let the non-melodic RH notes interrupt the singing melody.

- Linger on the interesting harmonic (chord) progression in measures 27–28, as the main theme reasserts itself the final time.

❧ TRANSPOSE

- *Ice Gliding* is written in ____ _____.

- Transpose measures 1–8 to F major, hands separately.

❧ CREATE

Imagine that *Ice Gliding* is being played by a string and woodwind ensemble (group).
What instruments would play the RH melody?
The other RH notes?   The LH?
Could the instruments change for measures 17–24?   How?

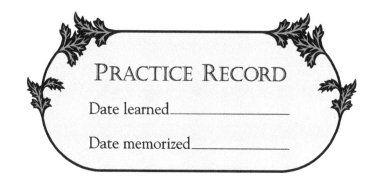

PRACTICE RECORD

Date learned_____

Date memorized_____

omposer Facts

(Paolo) Guiseppe (Gioacchino) Concone
(1801–1861), Italian, was mainly known as a teacher of singing as well as a composer of vocal studies and other pieces for singers, including two operas. He also was an organist and choir master as well as a composer of piano studies.

Ice Gliding

Op. 24, No. 23

Guiseppe Concone

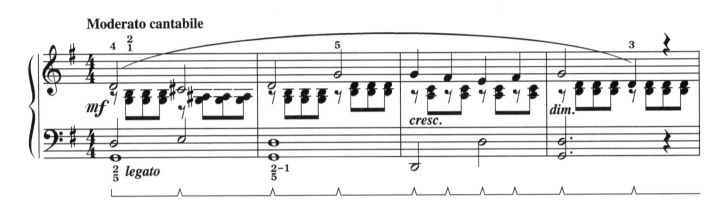

∞ BEFORE YOU PLAY

- On the keyboard, block the patterns of three sixteenth notes in measures 1–14.

  Example:

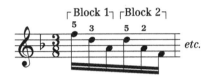

- Tap measures 25–48 hands together as you count aloud.

∞ AS YOU PLAY

- In measures 1–14 and measures 52–65, there is a feeling of two "big" beats per measure in the RH.

  In the LH of some measures (e.g. measures 1–2, etc.), there is a feeling of three "small" beats per measure.

  This creates a rhythmic ambiguity that adds energy and a feeling of restlessness.

- Listen to bring out the calm melodic character in the *Trio* (measures 25–51).

∞ TRANSPOSE

- *Scherzo* is written in ____ minor.
- Transpose the RH of measures 1–16 to E minor.

∞ CREATE

Scherzo is a very dramatic piece. Make up a descriptive title and story that fits the music.

Title:

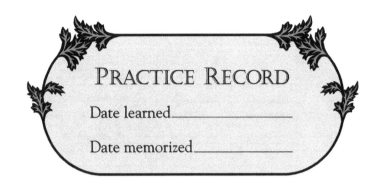

PRACTICE RECORD

Date learned_____

Date memorized_____

Composer Facts

Cornelius Gurlitt (1820–1901), *see page 10.*

Scherzo

Cornelius Gurlitt

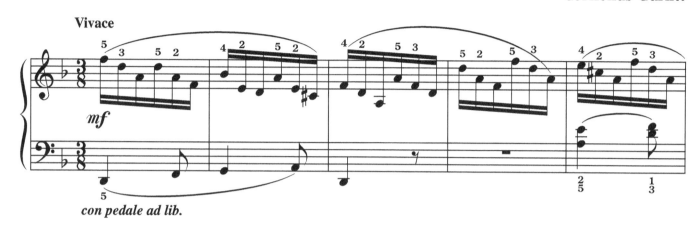

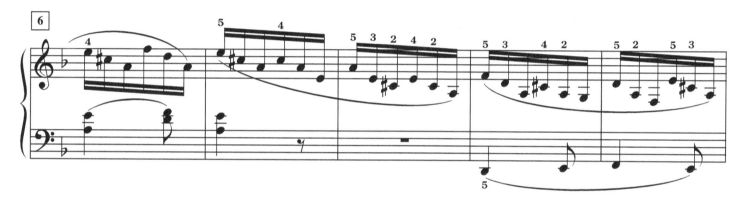

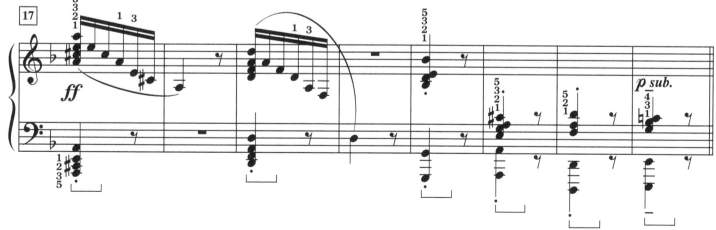

40

✎ BEFORE YOU PLAY

On the closed key cover, practice the octave tremolos (broken octaves) for LH, then RH. Keep the wrists level, arms relaxed, and fingers barely moving above the surface of the keys. The motion should be as small as possible. Make sure that elbows and wrists do not become tight.

✎ AS YOU PLAY

- Listen for even octave tremolos.
- Bring out the half-step movement (LH— measures 5–7, RH—measures 18–20).
- Make your playing bold and confident in measures 13–16 and measures 29–32.

✎ TRANSPOSE

- *The Curtain Rises* is written in B♭ minor.
- Transpose measures 1–16 to C minor, hands separately.

✎ CREATE

Reverse the order of the notes for each octave tremolo throughout, so that the upper note is always played first.

Example:

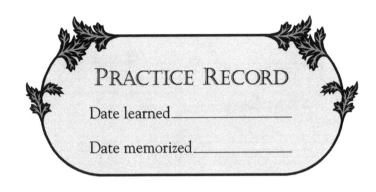

Composer Facts

Johann Wilhelm Hässler (1747–1822), German, was an organist, pianist and teacher who knew C. P. E. Bach (1714–1788) and Wolfgang Amadeus Mozart (1756–1791). Almost all of his compositions were written for the keyboard.

The Curtain Rises

Op. 49, No. 2

Johann Wilhelm Hässler

BEFORE YOU PLAY

On the closed key cover, "play" the RH alone. Use a gentle finger "pull" (toward the palm) for the repeated notes. Do not bounce the arm.

AS YOU PLAY

Listen for crisp, light *staccato* notes and a bright, joyous sound.

TRANSPOSE

• *Triumphal Fanfare* is written in ____ _____.

• Transpose it to F minor, the parallel minor key. Remember to raise the seventh (E♭), one half step, to E.

CREATE

Improvise (make up) your own four-measure fanfare by using repeated notes and broken chords.

PRACTICE RECORD

Date learned_____

Date memorized_____

omposer Facts

Jean-Baptiste Duvernoy (1800–1880), French, was the composer of several hundred piano pieces and studies. His Op. 176 is a particularly effective and even charming approach to the etude genre.

Triumphal Fanfare
Op. 176, No. 25

Jean-Baptiste Duvernoy

46

Glossary

TEMPO

a tempo	return to the tempo, especially after *rit.* or *accel.*
allegretto	a little fast and lively; a little slower than *allegro*
allegro	fast and lively
allegro assai	very fast; in 18th century music, sometimes means rather fast
allegro moderato	moderately fast and lively
allegro robusto	fast and lively, with boldness
allegro vivace	fast and lively, with life
con moto	with motion
moderato	moderate (medium) tempo
più mosso	more motion
rallentando (rall.)	gradually slowing, same as *rit.*
tempo primo	return to the first tempo
un poco agitato	a little agitated; a little excited
vivace	vivacious and brisk

DYNAMICS

accent (>) ♩ ♩	play this note louder than those around it
crescendo molto	gradually becoming much louder
forte-piano (fp)	loud, followed immediately by soft
fortissimo (ff)	very loud
fortississimo (fff)	very, very loud
forzando (fz or *ffz)*	very forced, very accented (same as *forzato*)
forzato (fz or *ffz)*	very forced, very accented (same as *forzando*)
pianissimo (pp)	very soft
pianississimo (ppp)	very, very soft
piano subito (p sub.)	suddenly soft
poco a poco crescendo	become louder, little by little
sforzando (sf)	a sudden, strong accent (same as *sforzato*)
sforzato (sfz)	a sudden, strong accent (same as *sforzando*)

Glossary (continued)

❧ ARTICULATIONS

legato	smooth and connected
portato	halfway between *legato* and *staccato*; "long" *staccato*
slur (⌣)	a curved line over or under notes that means to play *legato*
staccato (.)	to play detached (not *legato*); disconnected
staccatissimo (ᵛ)	very detached
tenuto (–)	hold the note(s) the full length; slight stress

❧ OTHER

ad lib. (libitum)	at the pleasure of the performer
calando	becoming softer; sometimes also slower
cantando	singing (same as *cantabile*)
come primo	as at first
con pedale	with pedal
con rubato	with small, temporary, expressive variations in tempo
dolce	sweetly
dolente	sorrowful; sadly
etude	a study; a piece that has a technical purpose
frish und munter	brisk and jolly
giocoso	playful, humorous
grazioso	gracefully
leggiero (also leggero) (legg.)	lightly
marziale	martial
misterioso	mysteriously
molto	much
octave sign (8ᵛᵃ)	play an octave higher or lower than written
ped. simile	continue pedaling in similar fashion as previously marked
più	more
poco	little
risoluto	bold; with determination
sempre	always
simile	continue in the same manner
sotto	under (as in "to play one hand under the other")
subito	suddenly
transpose	to play in a different key (pattern); the intervals remain the same, but the actual notes change
trill (∿)	a rapid alternation of a note with the one a 2nd above; different rules of execution apply, depending on the historic period of composition as well as the style
trio	the middle section in a minuet or scherzo; a piece in three parts; a group of three musicians